If You Could Wear My Sneakers!

POEMS BY

ART BY

SHEREE FITCH • DARCIA LABROSSE

FIREFLY BOOKS

A FIREFLY BOOK

Cataloging in Publication Data

Fitch, Sheree
If you could wear my sneakers!

Poems.
ISBN 1-55209-275-5 (bound)   ISBN 1-55209-259-3 (pbk.)

I. Labrosse, Darcia II. Title.

PS8561.I8614 1998   jC811'.54   C98-930892-8
PZ7.F57If 1998

Published in the United States in 1998
by Firefly Books (U.S.) Inc.
P.O. Box 1338, Ellicott Station
Buffalo, New York, USA
14205

With gratitude to Noel Kinsella
a right fighter
and a fighter for writers

—Sheree

With love to
Loup-Noé, Eden, Pacifique, Amandine, and Judith

—Darcia

Printed and bound in Canada

Introduction

I was seven years old when I wrote my first poem and discovered that words could make people laugh. That's when I started to dream about growing up to be a writer. I didn't even think that was a possibility, because where I lived there weren't any writers. But my dream came true.

I have spent most of my adult life trying to make sense of the world — and what it means to be human — by writing, it is the joy of tasting words on the tip of my tongue, the fun in the lip-slippery syllables of nonsense, and the swerve and curve of words spilling through the air that delights me most.

When UNICEF approached me to write a book of poems connected to the United Nations Convention on the Rights of the Child, I thought it could not be done. Nonsense was nonsense after all, and children's rights were important. But one morning in my writing room, the "Eloquent Young Elephant" paid me a visit. Really! I knew when I had finished the poem that I had figured out a way to do this book.

These poems do not "teach" rights. They are meant to be enjoyed as poems and then, I hope, to start a discussion between children and adults about issues that affect the lives of children around the world. Understanding there are rights that protect children is one step forward. Knowing that with rights come responsibility is another step. And turning our hopes and dreams into action is a leap we all can make.

I am honored to have been commissioned to write poetry that asks big questions about our world. I hope you have fun with these poems — and ask lots of questions too. I would like a safe place for every child in this world. Maybe if we all ask questions and work toward a solution, there will one day be peace in our hearts, our lives and our world. That young elephant told me it could be more than "just a dream".

After all, dreams do come true. Otherwise I would not be writing this letter to you on the day I leave for Africa! That's another dream I had a long time ago....

Sheree Fitch

Table of Contents

If You Could Wear My Sneakers!

If you were me
And I were you
For just a day
Or maybe two
Then maybe you
And maybe me
Would see the me
That you were too

Because...
The you I see
You try to be
Never ever
Speaks to me

See...
If you knew
The me I am
Or I could know
The you you be
I think we would
Eventually
Discover we liked
Broccoli!

Yeah...
We could form
The broccoli bunch
Invite each other
Out to lunch
Share our little
Broccoli trees
Cover them
With melted cheese

But...
You pass me by
Without a smile
As if I were
A crocodile
Then look the other
Way in case
You see the me
That's in my face

If you could wear my sneakers
(You might have to plug your nose)
And if I could wear your shoes
(Even if they crunched my toes)
Maybe we could see the us
We never got to meet
The you and me
That might have found
More broccoli
To eat

Speaking of Speaking

Does...
An otter utter in Ottanese?
A panda prattle in Pandanese?
A gerbil gabble in Gerbilese?
A jerboa jabber in Jerboanese?
A quetzel quarrel in Quetzanese?
A baboon babble in Baboonese?
A cat chat in Siamese?
A yak yack in Yakanese?
A hippo harrumph in Hippotamese?

Well...
Whatever the language
Of this, that or these
A sneeze
is a... a...
Sneeze
is a... a...
Sneeze
is a
SNEEZE!

(Use a tissue, s'il vous please!)

To Each a Home

I'll be back to my hive by five
Because I'm a bumblebee

I'll be back to my tree by three
Because I'm a chickadee

I'll be back to my den by ten
Because I'm a bear, you see

I'll be back to my pad in a tad
I'm a frog on a log in a bog

I'll be back when I get the bug
Said the sluggish slug with a shrug

I'm back
For wherever I roam
My dome of a home
Comes along

And Who Are You?

My name is...
Alphonse Alawishes
Abadaba
Bertie Bingo
Corky Coolguy
Dippy Dingle
Eenie Eater
Fenton Fergus
Georgie Ghengis
Harry Horton
Ian Ivy
Jumpy Jordan
Koola Kala
Lucky Loonie
Momba Mellow
Fly-a-Kite Mike
Naughty Neville
Onward Orville
Peter Pickle
Quirky Quentin
Rascal Randy
RaRaRa Raccoon!
Sweetie Sugar
Sisboombah

Twirly Tuba
Tony
Understumble Underwort
Victor Voickle Valentine
Wrinkled Willywhoops
Xylophonist Xaxafrax
Yikes the Yingy Yang
Zat's all

You might think it
A strange name
You might think it long
But you know what?
It's my name
Every name is a song

And who, may I ask, are you?

The Gnu-Ewe-Cockatoo-Emu All Are Welcome Crew

I knew an emu
He knew an emu too
We all flew together
We became the Emu Crew

Then what do you know?
Along came a gnu
Who said, "I'm not an emu
But I want to join too."

Then the next thing you know
The Emu Crew grew
We had to start anew
As the Gnu-Emu Crew

Then a gnu asked a cockatoo
Who asked another two
Our membership expanded
How our happy crew grew

And that's the way it was until...
We all met a ewe

Now I guess you probably know
That ewes have joined us too
(When we all get together
There's a hundred and fifty-two)

But perhaps you did not know
That our name had to grow
It is true we never knew
That the old Emu Crew

Would some day be known far and wide
As The One and Only
Gnu-Ewe-Cockatoo-Emu
All Are Welcome Crew!

And...
We've just received an application
From a dancing kangaroo

The Stinky Truth

"What do you think?
Do you think that I stink?"
Said the skunk
"Do you thunk that I smell?"
"Well, I think that you stink
But I think for a skunk
That you smell
Incredibly
Well."

Dr. P. Uffin

I've a yearning
That is burning
A desire for
Higher learning
I would like
To go to college
To improve upon
My knowledge
I've heard words
Are for the birds
I have looked
In many books
(I know
I can't get by
If I'm depending
On my looks)
Intellectual stimulation!
Cerebellum circulation!
Please accept
My registration
I'll be the first
Of my relations
To get
My education

(I have heard
There is no fee
That I get
To go for free)
You won't be laughin'
At this puffin
Who now knows that
She knows nothin'
When I've learned
My ABCs
What an abecedarian
Puffin I'll be
Then I'll get
My PhD
In puffin
Prose and
Poetry

16

The Beagle and the Beluga and the Eagle's Fine Times

I know a beagle
Who loved bagels
In fact he loved to beg for bagels
In fact he wagged his tail for bagels
And haggled for those bagels
Whenever bugles blew

One day the beagle met a beluga
Who played the boogie-woogie-bugle
The beagle giggled, "Hi beluga!"
Then blew a jig with his kazoo

Then the beagle and the beluga
Eating bagels, blowing bugles
Met an eagle who was eager
To eat some buttered bagels too

So the beagle and the eagle
And the bugle-playing beluga
Sailed together and saw the seven million
Wonders of the world

It was
A Boondoggling
Mindboggling
Hornswoggling
Time

They played
The Boogie-Woogie
Beluga-Eager
Eagle-beagle
Blues

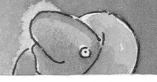

17

The Giraffe Who Could Not Laugh

There was a giraffe
Who had a laugh
Stuck half-way down his throat
No matter how hard he tried
He could not giggle it out
It began as the snort
That grew into the laugh
That got caught in the neck
Of that poor giraffe
What an awful guffaw!
What a choke of a joke!
Help! he yelled
To the animal folk
As the laugh got as big
As a bubblegum bubble
Enough! he sniffed
Which doubled his trouble
    But...
The animal folk formed a laughter
brigade
    They brought food
    They brought water
    They brought first aid
"Hold still, if you will,"
Said the lion in command

"I know what to do
I have a long range plan."
The giraffe was nervous
He turned extremely pale
The lion tickled his belly
With a *SWISH!*
Of his tail
Then...
With a ha! With a ho! With a hee! hee! hee!
The giggle wiggled out
And that laugh was free!
Where did it go?
A eucalyptus tree
Now the giraffe only laughs
When his friends are close by
That is why giraffes
Hold their heads up high

The Way It Is

Why doth the sloth
Moveth so slow?
Why doth the sloth
Have three sloth toes?
Why doth the sloth
Hangeth upside down?
Why doth he?
The sloth is
Just *weird*, I suppoth

I sayeth! saith the sloth
I am slow because
That's the way it is
The way it was
My three toes doth

What three toes do
I'm as happy for me
As you are for you
And the wayeth the world
Spinneth upside down?
It's just different, not weird
My sky is your ground
And if-eth you thinketh
That faster is better
I sayeth to you
That it doesn't much matter
For if you're a sloth
Slow seemeth just fine
You doeth things your way
I'll doeth things mine

Too Much Too Soon

A busy beaver got a fever
So an elder was called
He looked the beaver over and said
I am saddened and appalled!

This little beaver has been working
Far too long
Hasn't anybody noticed that
He isn't very strong?

I suggest lots of rest
Lots of time in the sun
Every day he must play
Lots of time just for fun

When the beaver's older
Then he can be employed
He's really much too young
Youth must be enjoyed

So now the beaver's better
He plays the way
All beavers would
And...

He tries to keep his lodge cleaned up
Like every beaver should

Whoa!

NO!
squabbling
or
nibbling
no
scratching
or
clawing
no calling
me names
that bite
i
n
t
o
my
heart

YES!

listening
yes
sharing
yes
nuzzling
yes
caring
just loving me
right from
the start

The Eloquent Young Elephant

Did you hear the elephants
Trumpeting last night?
They thundered past my bedroom
The earth rumbled back in fright

They were going to fight a battle
Thump-galumphing off to war
Did you hear a wee small voice say
What are we fighting for?

Did you see the elephant kerfuffle
As they stopped marching on?
A toppled pile of elephants
A jungle tangle until dawn

As they were unravelling
Their tails and trunks and ears
They had a chance to listen
Did you have a chance to hear?

The smallest of the elephants
The one who'd asked, "What for?"
Crawled out from underneath and said
"I will not go to war!"

"I may be young but listen
I'm old enough to know
If I go on to battle
I might...
Die."

Well...
You could have heard the moon cry
As the night continued on
As that elephant elaborated
On what was right and wrong

Did you see the older elephants
Start to twitch their trembling ears?
Did you see those elder elephants
Weep enormous tears?
Did you think they'd flood the jungle
And we'd all float out to sea?
(I was a little worried—
I'm a fretful chimpanzee)

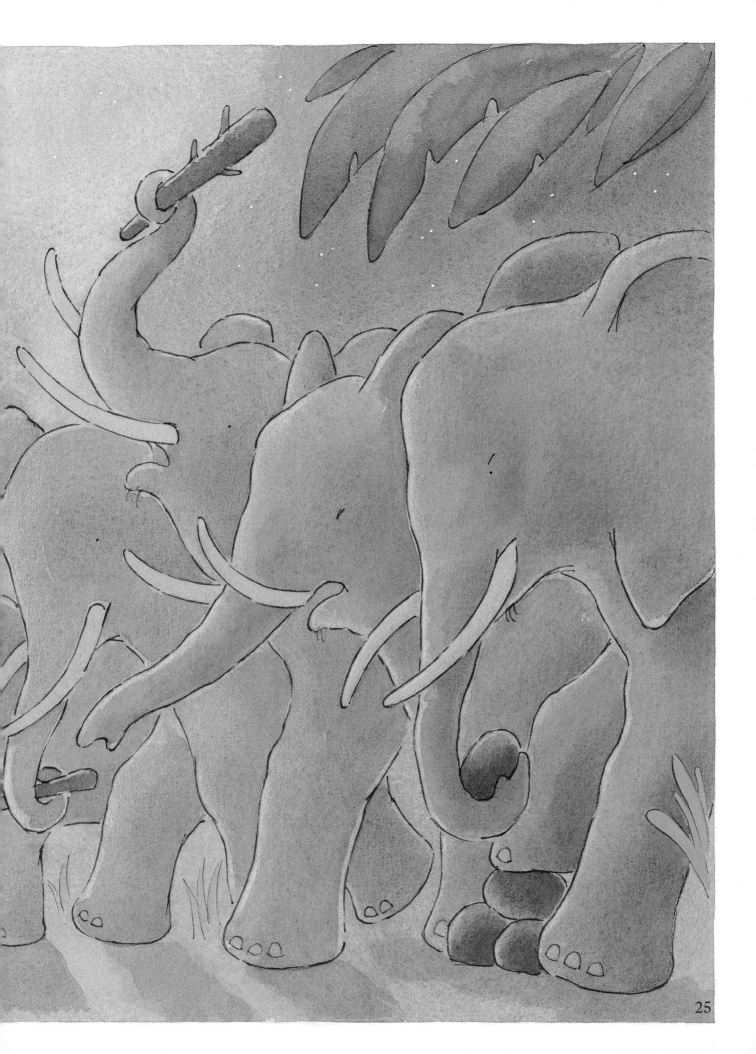

Did you hear their snozzles snivelling
A sound like thunder through a hose
You have to plug your ears when
An elephant blows his nose
(And there must have been a hundred
More or less, I suppose)

Then...
Did you see the early morning sun
Come shining through the trees
In a leafy shadow dance
In the early morning jungle breeze?

As the elephants turned homewards
With the smallest in the lead
Did you hear them sing a song of
The smallest's greatest deed?

Their trunks had turned from trumpets
That had been sounding off for war
Into flutes and pipes and piccolos
That played of peace forever more

Do you know it really happened?
As wild as it might seem
The youngest was the wisest
And peace was not a dream

Secrets

Some things are for telling
Some things are for yelling
Some things are for whispering
To flowers or the sky
Other secrets wing their way
To light by and by

Shine, Shine, Shine

One little firefly
In a jar
Lovely lonely
Fallen star

One little firefly
Flying free
Shining star
In a galaxy

Do You Know Your Rights?

WHICH RIGHT IS RIGHT?

Match the poem on the left to the correct "right" that it tells on the next page.
Answers page 32.

And Who Are You?

Speaking of Speaking

To Each a Home

Whoa!

Dr. P. Uffin

The Stinky Truth

Secrets

If You Could Wear My Sneakers!

The Gnu-Ewe-Cockatoo-Emu All Are Welcome Crew

The Way It Is

Too Much Too Soon

The Beagle, the Beluga and the Eagle's Fine Times

The Eloquent Young Elephant

Shine, Shine, Shine

The Giraffe Who Could Not Laugh

You have the right to an education (Article 28).

∎

You have the right to enough food, clean water, health care and shelter (Article 27).

∎

You have the right to privacy (Article 16).

∎

You have the right to play (Article 31).

∎

You have the right to a name and nationality (Article 7).

∎

You have the right to be protected from abuse (Article 19).

∎

If you are disabled, you have the right to special care to help you grow up in the same way as other children (Article 23).

∎

You have these rights no matter what; all children do (Article 2).

∎

You have the right to be protected from war (Article 38).

You have the right to enjoy your own culture, language and religion (Article 30).

∎

You have the right to say what you think, and give information to others, unless it gets in the way of others' rights (Article 13).

∎

You have the right to fair treatment by the law (Article 37).

∎

You have the right to meet, make friends and join clubs, unless it gets in the way of others' rights (Article 15).

∎

You have the right to give your opinion in matters that affect you, and adults have to take it seriously (Article 12).

∎

You have the right to receive the highest standard of health and medical care possible (Article 24).

∎

You have the right to be protected from work that damages your health or gets in the way of school (Article 32).

And Who Are You?
Article 7: Children have the right to
a name and nationality.

Speaking of Speaking
Article 30: Children, especially of minority and
indigenous populations, have the
right to practice their own culture,
religion and language.

To Each A Home
Article 27: Children have the right
to a standard of living adequate for
their physical, mental, spiritual,
moral and social development.

Whoa!
Article 19: Children have the right
to protection from abuse, neglect
and violence.

Dr. P. Uffin
Article 28: Children have the right to
an education, including free primary education.

The Stinky Truth
Article 13: Children have the right
to obtain and share information,
and to express their opinions.

Secrets
Article 16: Children have the right
to protection from interference in
privacy, family and home.

If You Could Wear My Sneakers!
Article 2: All rights apply to all children
without exception.

The Gnu-Ewe-Cockatoo-Emu All Are Welcome Crew
Article 15: Children have the right
to meet with others and to join or
form associations.

The Way It Is
Article 23: Disabled children have
the right to special care to enjoy a
full life in dignity.

Too-Much, Too Soon
Article 32: Children have the right
to be protected from labour that is exploitative,
or damaging to their
health and education.

The Beagle and the Beluga and the Eagle's Fine Times
Article 31: Children have the right to leisure,
play and participation in
cultural and artistic activities.

The Eloquent Young Elephant
Article 12: Children have the right
to express their opinions, and to have these
opinions taken into account in matters affecting
them; and
Article 38: Children have the right
to be protected from war.

Shine Shine Shine
Article 37: Children have the right to fair
treatment by the law.

The Giraffe Who Could Not Laugh
Article 24: Children have the right to the
highest standard of health and medical
care attainable.

To explore the UN Convention on the Rights of the Child further, contact your local UNICEF office or UNICEF headquarters for curriculum guides, posters, videos and other learning resources for home or school.